come-hither
honeycomb

Also by Erin Belieu

Poetry

Slant Six

Black Box

One Above & One Below

Infanta

As Editor

The Extraordinary Tide: New Poetry by American Women
(with Susan Aizenberg)

come-hither honeycomb

poems by

erin belieu

COPPER CANYON PRESS

PORT TOWNSEND, WASHINGTON

Cover art: Whiskey Radish

Copper Canyon Press is in residence at Fort Worden State Park in Port Townsend, Washington, under the auspices of Centrum. Centrum is a gathering place for artists and creative thinkers from around the world, students of all ages and backgrounds, and audiences seeking extraordinary cultural enrichment.

LIBRARY OF CONGRESS CATALOGING-IN-PUBLICATION DATA
Names: Belieu, Erin, author.
Title: Come-hither honeycomb : poems / by Erin Belieu.
Description: Port Townsend, Washington : Copper Canyon Press, [2021] |
Summary: "A collection of poems by Erin Belieu"—Provided by
publisher.
Identifiers: LCCN 2020030147 | ISBN 9781556596100 (paperback)
Subjects: LCGFT: Poetry.
Classification: LCC PS3552.E479 C66 2021 | DDC 811/.54—dc23
LC record available at https://lccn.loc.gov/2020030147

98765432 FIRST PRINTING

COPPER CANYON PRESS
Post Office Box 271
Port Townsend, Washington 98368
www.coppercanyonpress.org

Acknowledgments

Grateful acknowledgment goes to the publications in which these poems originally appeared (sometimes under different titles or in different versions):

Academy of American Poets Poem-a-Day: "Dum Spiro Spero," "Pity the Doctor, Not the Disease," and "She Returns to the Water"; *The American Poetry Review:* "In Which a Therapist Asks for the Gargoyle Who Sits on My Chest"; *The Ekphrastic Writer: Creating Art-Influenced Poetry, Fiction and Nonfiction,* Janée J. Baugher: "Sundays"; *The Evansville Review:* "The Man Who Fills In Space"; *Kenyon Review:* "Instructions for the Hostage"; *Narrative:* "Hypotenuse" (previously "The Trees Named Glowing Embers") and "In Airports"; *Poetry:* "Loser Bait"; *T: The New York Times Style Magazine:* "Your Failure"; *Willow Springs:* "When I Am a Teenage Boy"; *Women's Review of Books: "Please Forgive Me All That I Have Ruined—"*

My gratitude to the dear friends whose poetry inspired me in the making of this book: Mark Bibbins, Chris Hayes, Keith Kopka, Dana Levin, Cate Marvin, Adrian Matejka, Carl Phillips, Kevin Prufer, and Ann Townsend. With thanks to Debbie Gary, whose generosity (and airplane hangar) allowed me the space to finish this book.

Always, for Jude

She notices something then that has caught on her sleeve. It is the tiniest of feathers, hardly more than a wisp of down. She detaches it carefully, meaning to inspect it more closely, but it is so slight that she cannot keep hold of it. She sees it only for an instant before the wind takes it, a thread of brightness that shivers from her fingertips and is gone.

from Paraic O'Donnell's *The Maker of Swans*

Contents

come-hither
honeycomb

Instructions for the Hostage

You must accept the door is never shut.
You're always free to leave at any time,
though the hostage will remain, no matter what.

The damage could be managed, so you thought.
Essential to the theory of your crime:
you must accept the door is never shut.

Soon, you'll need to choose which parts to cut
for proof of life, then settle on your spine—
though the hostage will remain, no matter what.

Buried with a straw, it's the weak who start
considering their price. You're no great sum.
You must accept the door was never shut

and make a half-life there, aware, apart,
afraid your captor's lost you, so far down,
though the hostage you'll remain, no matter what.

Blink once for yes, and twice for yes—the heart
makes a signal for the willing, its purity sublime.
You must accept the door is never shut,
though the hostage will remain, no matter what.

Loser Bait

Some of us
are chum.

Some of us
are the come-hither
honeycomb

gleamy in the middle
of the trap's busted smile.

Though I let myself a little
off this hook, petard
by which I flail,

and fancy myself more
flattered—
no ugly worm!

Humor me
as hapless nymph,
straight outta *Bulfinch's,* minding
my own beeswax,

gamboling, or picking flowers
(say daffodils),

doing that unspecified stuff
nymphs do
with their hours,

until spied by a layabout youth,
or a rapey god
who leaps unerring, stag-like,
quicker than smoke, to the wrong idea.

Or maybe
the right?

For didn't I supply
the tippy box, too?
Notch the stick on which
to prop it?

Didn't I fumble the clove hitch
for the rope?
Leave the trip lying obvious
in the tall, buggy grass?

Ever it was.
Duh.

Be the mat,
and the left foot finds you welcome.

Though there's always a subject, a him-
or herself. But to name it
calls it down, like Satan
or the IRS.

It must be swell,
to have both deed and
the entitlement, for leaners who hold our lien,

consumers who consume like
red tide ripping through a coastal lake.

Who find themselves so very *well*
when gazing in that kiddie pool, or any
skinny inch of water.

That guy, remember? How tell this tale
without him? A story
so hoary, his name's Pre-Greek.

What brought Narcissus down?
A spotty case
of the disdains, I think,

a one-man performance
wherein the actor hates his audience.

Pity the Doctor, Not the Disease

Science in its tedium reveals that every spirit
we spirit ganks a solid half hour from

our life spans. So says my doctor, a watery,

Jesus-eyed man, and hard to suffer
with his well-intended scrips for yoga

and neti pots, notably stingy with the better

drugs, in situ here amid the disinfected
toys, dreadful in their plastic baskets.

Above his head, the flayed men of medical
illustration are nailed for something like

décor. The eyeball scheme is best,

with its wondrous canal of Schlemm,
first favorite of all weirdly name-

saked body parts. It's just a splotch
of violet on the diagram, but without it

our aqueous humors would burst
their meshy dams and overflow. *Dust*

thou art, to dust returnest, was not spoken
of the soul . . . is what I quote to him

as he thumps my back with his tiny
doctor's tomahawk. But he's used to me.

We have an understanding. What he
means to miser, I've come to spend

most lavishly. And I feel fortunate again
to be historically shaky in the maths,
enough to avoid making an easy sum

of my truly happy hours, or nights curled

sulfurous on my side, a priced-to-sell
shrimp boiling in anxious sleep.

If we're lucky, it's always a terrible time

to die. Better the privilege of booze
than the whim of one more shambolic

butcher shelling peasants in a wood,
our world's long spree of Caesars

starting wars to pay their bills
in any given era's Rome. Turns out,

Longfellow's stomach did for him,
and he died thirsty, calling for more opium.

Free of the exam room now, I spot the same

busted goldfish in his smeary bowl
beside the door where he's glugged along

for years, a mostly failed distraction

for poxed or broken children. I raise my fin
to him, celebrate the poison we're all

swimming in, remembering the way
you say cheers in Hungarian:

Isten, Isten, meaning,
in translation, "I'm a god. You're a god."

In Airports

It was the season for
weeping   in airports for walking

and bleeding   in airports—

the white corridors   their rocking
chairs,   the ghosts   and trains   and strangers
all overcast   the windows

and buzzing   of people   and
earbuds   always the weather   in airports

a stranger season   she never knew—

It was the season   for these and   (what?)
the lady said   standing behind
the long white counter

and hives   and sores

what left their   weeping   nettled prints
below her clothes

red   like the ghost   of maple
leaves   raked wet   from the sidewalk—

It was the season   of storm delays

and lightning clocks
of . . . *shame*   and ghosts   on trains   hanging

from   the vinyl straps   clinging to   the stainless
poles   or buzzing in   the long white rows   of rocking
chairs   in airports—

a stranger season   she never knew

—what was gone   and where   and buzzing
how it walked   and wailing   like

a ghost . . . a *shame*   was something   the lady said
standing behind   the long white counter

. . . a *shame*   she said   and looked concerned—

She heard her   (what?)   a stranger said
and never knew—

being   always the weather   in airports

the season   the weeping   a wet buzzing
sore   she walked   on board . . . a *shame*

a lady   gone—   a stranger   flew

Your Failure

was mostly predictable
            and daily,

like the wee, fluorescent lizards
            still creeping greenly
                        along the front doorframe,

who think a house the image of
            escape, despite how clear the world
                        is just behind them.

Who, wasting, never know
            we never mean to trap them.
                        We try to help.

But God, it's tough to take,
            this animal made complete
                        from dumb instinct,

the urge that drives them,
            steadily amiss,
                        constant, and unfair;

it hurts to watch them
            scramble, dewlaps throbbing,
                        the Swiss precision of their fear.

Now sorting out the wreck,
          she digs her broom into another
                    hidden, grubby crack,

to find the husk
          these creatures leave us
                    because of what they lack.

When I Am a Teenage Boy

I am like my parents' house, in a state
of constant remodel we can ill afford,
the noise behind a tarp producing little more

than dust. But the footprint must change
despite great expense. Large parts
need to move for the sake of *flow*. I learn

the trick is to appear intact, though recently
the problem of my torso is introduced.
My mother says I've always been *a little*

Jew around the waist. She had specific
hopes, shelled out for the stag tuxedo suit,
sent me for cotillion lessons. Mind like

a boardwalk jewelry store, heyday 1962,
she wears her hostess gown in the kitchen
while I creak along with the Crock-Pot

pulverizing our Sunday stew. Because
I'm an only, she put a TV in my room
for company. It's a solid business, taping cable

porn to VHS. But when I'm caught extorting
the gym coach, meds are discussed at school.
My mother says we don't do meds,

my dad and me. And I'm not caught often.
Who would I be without this brain that twitches
like the dragonflies I hose from the pool's filter?

Instead, I take myself in hand. I buy a trench
with birthday money sent by a childless aunt
we thought dead years ago. We don't use

the word "lesbian" because, my mother says,
Who says that sort of thing? I perform my coat
darkly in a graveyard split by an interstate, where

our housekeeper's son is housed. Here, I feel most
vivid, futurely, Peter Parker praying for his spider.
Oh, I am replete with plans. I'll be like that prince

in the novel I didn't read for English class.
I don't finish books, but I get the gist—
some sad lady who offs herself by train. Ballrooms.

A bunch of Russians suffering. Blah blah.
But that guy Stiva eating his sausages? Someday
I'll have a faithful servant, too. Or at least a wife.

I fear I'll always be a little piggy in the middle,
but that grease I'll lick from my fingers?
It tastes like everything now.

Hypotenuse

Sapling maple
bit in the neck

by a weed
whacker—
a tree called

Glowing Embers
for leaves
that simmer like

coals in a grate,

one of three we
bought for the top
of the yard.

Little footage,
this plot, where
it thrived, at first,

then ghosted
away; a *spectre,*
tree shaped.

A *trace . . .*

Now, flowering
vines, chosen
not for sweetness

but disguise,

throttle our
spineless chimney.
Fire ants,

unchecked, build
small volcanoes
to the door.

Now,
the cats who
persist in

the yard's
drainage ditch
visit me

where I sit
on my porch,

a vigil with no
body, before
no sun.

Minor demons,

these familiars
refuse to be
touched,

having learned
their certain distance:

two fixed points
    =
the length
of belonging

to no one.

The Man Who Fills In Space

. . . and from the moment that everything is limitless, what remains?

Guy de Maupassant, "Letter from a Madman"

The man who fills in space is petrified.

The outlines of each table, counter,
his and the spouse's nightstands, all blur
beneath the mess of his collections.

Covering his mouth, the man
often yawns reflexively.
It's hard to feel your own unease
so tedious, a house too quiet.

And he is growing weightless,
churlish, lapsing into sulks, as the bees
that work inside him plot more often
to refuse him the lullabying

comfort of their swarm.
But when he pokes the canker
of that great, blank whatever
he never hopes to find, he swears

he hears it laugh, the terrible what
of what is not. It yawns
right back at him.

The man who fills in space
drips with the stalagmites
he fashions for his temple—

pillars made from leisure magazines,
sour-smelling foreign change, a plastic bag
engorged with dead men's wallets,

the treasure of his mother's
broken Seal-a-Meal—

all the stuff of him
pressed lovingly beneath a pelt
of dust in which he sometimes thinks
to write his name.

And when he leaves each night
to make himself less awfully not,

and drinks to make the bees return,
searching for the necessary spot
from which to phone his mistress,

sometimes the moon comes by,
peering through the window of his car
to wonder at this man who fills in space.

And the man looks back at her,
marveling at how lonely she must be,

those barren miles, the nothing
of a few golf balls, a clutch of silent
flags planted in her porous white.

Though he recalls the astronaut who left
a tiny silver pin behind, proving
someone he can't remember claimed

another place he'll never go.

The man who fills in space,
he thinks of this
while considering the moon—the sadness

of the object, that single, sharp prick
alone somewhere in the universe.

Dum Spiro Spero

Come Lord, and lift the fallen bird
Abandoned on the ground;
The soul bereft and longing so
To have the lost be found.

Before the movers came,
we found the sparrows' nest

concealed inside the chive
plant on the patio.

And the bald chicks there
calling, unfledged, undone.

Love, the mean days collecting
scored us, and hourly

such years: we feel too much

assembling what our world
got wrong—black artery

of wires, branched hazard, rat
stinking in the beams. Wrong as

your mattress on your mother's
floor, a cheap construction,
walls where the only studs

are the anchor of your grief.

Take this distance as you go,
Love, which is my faith, tedious,

steady, like scraping gum
from a shoe. Strong as a cobweb,

I give you this durable string.

Because I remember you,
who save the sparrows;

the chicks calling and calling
and you who won't forget them;

have seen the ghost who rents
your eyes dissolve when
your face turns to the light.

Today, I watched the other birds
who lived this winter

peppering our tulip tree. The buds'
tough seams begin to crack.

Ordinary. No sign to read, I know.
But while we breathe, we hope.

Sundays

after church, she shucked the grip of shoes, peace beings
of neighbors, the puce-faced elders and pilly felt hangings,

and that soft, sad man with his sorrows,
no business of hers.

Looking up where he drooped, Where there's smoke, there's fire,
she thought, choosing one adult fib that seemed, for once, more

possible than not; she felt him contagious, a man with his torso
gouged like that, of no-thank-you troubles and terrible holes.

She was sorry for him, though decided their story likely a lie,
unlikely stories abounding, aplenty, for little girls to buy.

But she wanted no truck nonetheless, nuh uh—and what had she
done?—how bad could she be?—and whose son was this,

this sad, soft man another would hurt like that?
So Sundays, she shucked and ran and climbed,

the birch in her yard no scourge. Who'd put, she thought, a gift
worth having at the end of a whip? Such adult nonsense;

if she needed beseeching, here were the leaves now candling
their verdigris, in spring, where a girl could be redeemed,

only as sorry as she considered necessary, sewing herself into
what anyone who really looked could see was something true.

Reckless, she went, farther, higher, climbing clean into the birch's
crown, its limbs growing greener and thinner, the girl now certain

it was only a father who'd do that to a kid and call it a lesson.
How lovely that spirit,

this girl at the top, knowing no one could reach her.

Please Forgive Me   All That I Have Ruined—

is what I wrote in a letter   four years ago

and which   in retrospect   feels painfully
ridiculous   the lyric flourishes   absurd . . .

Though it isn't like   I didn't pony up   for all
my EXTRA.   I took that check   for every meal

always ready to confuse   the sum that someone
wants from me   with the balance   of myself.

                          *

My son and I   we've gotten good at being quiet
after all those years   of someone else's noise.   Not
unhappy quiet   but better than most   at keeping still.

It can feel willful at the holidays   when half the time
I'm left to herd   the silence on my own   but mostly
we ghost along contentedly   through our dailiness.

My son says he's convinced   if we were predators
we'd dive more silently than barn owls   who are
extremely silent   with feathers notched like steak knives

that break the air to make them so.   On other days
we are benign   slowly shifting from room to room   more
stealthy than giraffes   whom scientists believe   at most

emit a noncommittal hum   though their experiments can't

entirely decide.   Most often   drowning comes to us
like this: so very quietly   while those dithering in the boil
forget one decent option to consider: save yourself.

Once   my son went under   sneaky-like
right behind my back   when I was lifeguard for his Tiny
Tuna pre-K class.   Once   he vanished absolutely

inside a rack of discount dresses at a giant mall
pretending to hang there like an affordable   floral print.

He watched me call and call   my terror bursting
skyward   all glassy spangle and screech   a one-woman
fireworks display.   And because

he wasn't obviously damaged   I now take pleasure in
the thought of him   invisible inside those dearly
purchased minutes   loosed from the flaming dirigible

of my fear   the red balloon unknotted from his wrist.

*

Which is one kind of message sent by the universe
though   typically   uneasy to parse.   Like the cassowary

at Miami's dumpy zoo   unknown to us before
as a thoroughly accomplished killer   nature having
furnished it with good-size daggers on its middle toes

with which it's more than willing   when provoked
to unzip the human body like a duffel bag.

And how its minders came to us before
the aviary show   since we were closest to the stage

instructing us to hold   completely still   when
they brought it out   to tuck in our feet   and put
our hands deep into our pockets.   *Really*

they repeated   *completely still.*   But how

I envied it   that mindless dinosaur   caring
for nothing but the little gobs of meal its trainer
threw at the concrete stage   to keep it occupied.

How beautifully there/not there   the bird was
complete   unto itself   a savage trick I recognize
as having once perfected.   The truth is   I've lost

that gift.   In my early dotage   my edge begins
to bubble   creeping like the glass in a cathedral.
I weep easily   at stupid stuff.   The truth is   my son

only misses the dogs now.   The one with eyes
like ice in a glass   on a bar top   the other

unstoppable   who ate a lightbulb whole;   theirs
was such a loving   faithful chaos.   It was a thing
of joy for us   back then   to watch them run.

In Which a Therapist Asks for the Gargoyle
Who Sits on My Chest

Better say first,
the gargoyle she's requested,

I doubt he'll appear.

A fragrant character at most,
he's so wily, and hard to woo,

and God knows I'm terrible
at therapy—

the pushy box of tissues

and kindly on-the-clock
neutrality. It's exhausting,

how the whole's designed to scrub
our greasy pan of sorrows to
a gleam in which we've actually paid

to see ourselves. Caveat emptor?

Oh, verily.
To talk and talk like this is what
our age calls progress—

that peculiar human rage for moving
forward, like tourists walking off
of cliffs while taking selfies.

But since I've come to talk

where I'm urged to use my similes:
it's apt to say I *feel*
most like a Fenian incursion—

the third botched skirmish,
specifically. God bless the Irish

(those poets) for thinking they
could hotwire Canada, then sell it
to the British.

Though this makes perfect sense

to me, another unsurprising
outcome of an ill-considered plot,

conjured awkward in a haystack
near a town namesaked for that
rebellion's leader, one John O'Neill—

a man with such a gift for losing,
he finally thought he'd really rather
not die trying

(and proving, therapeutically,
it's best to recognize your limits).

Charged with speaking honestly,

I'll confide I think it late for
custom-order hindsight, or rigged

stories spat into our mouths when we
were only infants by the one bitchy
fairy not invited to the party.

What patterns there might be
emerged Cassandra-style,

with inner portents left
for me to sort, then artfully
ignore for half a century. Maybe that's

the weight we grown-ups mule, being
untranslated books the book club
never votes to read, its measure

heavy as the Easter Island glyphs of
Rongorongo, a mystery bitten into
wood by ancient shark teeth.

Maybe it's enough to recognize

ourselves unsolvable, half trash,
half glitter bomb, dropped along
the trench by dying stars.

The French say, *who can say?*

And since they basically invented
what we know of dread, and food,

and love, this seems a likely place
to make like Ginger Rogers

forever waltzing backward down
the stairs, partnered with a man
who never liked her—

that feathered, practiced creature,
bleeding in her heels,

her steps not what I'd call the act
of any faith, but more a process

of elimination. Until she finds
the bottom, searching for her mark,

while spinning toward the promised spots of light.

As for the Heart

I am come to the age
of pondering my lastness:

buying what seems likely
my final winter coat at Macy's,
or when a glossy magazine
(so very blithely)
asks me to *renew*. As for

my heart, that ever-pixilated
tweener, how tediously long
I've been expected to baby
her complaint
(unLOVED unLOVED),

alarmed and stubborn clock—
refusing to listen even as
the more intrepid tried.

Now she mostly mutters
to herself, though
occasionally there's
some clanging, a tinny sound,

like the radiator in a Southie
triple decker, fractious as
a pair of cowboy boots
in a laundromat's dryer.

It's always been
this joke the old ones know—
in such a state
of nearly doneness,

the world grows sweeter,
as if our later days
were underscored with music
from a nocturne's saddest
oboe hidden in the trees.

Just yesterday,
while standing in the kitchen,
my son complained nonstop
about his AP psych class
while wolfing warmed-up
bucatini from a crazed,
pink china bowl.

Shiny, kvetching creature.
Even if I could tell him
what he doesn't want to know,
I wouldn't. But now

the pissy storm that's spent
all afternoon flapping like
a dirty sheet
has wandered off
to spook some other
neighborhood.

There's one barbed weed
pushing up greenly through
my scruffy loropetalum.

And it falls on me, this little
cold rain the day has left.

She Returns to the Water

The dive starts
on the board . . .

something Steve
often said,

or *Rub some dirt*
in it, Princess,
when in his lesser

inscrutable mood;

Steve of the hair gel
and whistle; a man
who was her

diving coach,
who never seemed

to like her much.
Which was odd,

given, objectively,
her admirable discipline
and natural gifts,

the years and years
of practice, and the long

row of golden
trophies she won

for his team. The girl
she was then,

confused, partly
feral, like the outdoor
cat you feed

when you remember
to but won't allow

to come inside . . .

She's thinking of Steve
now, many years
later, while swimming

naked in her wealthy
landlord's pool. Or

"grotto," to call it
properly, an ugly,
Italian word for

something lovely,

ringed, as it is,
with red hibiscus;

white lights
in the mimosa trees

draping their blurry
pearls along
the water's skin.

It's three a.m.,

which seemed
the safest time for
this experiment,

in which she's turned
her strange and aging
body loose. Once,

a man she loved
observed, *You're
the kind of woman*

*who feels embarrassed
just standing in*

a room alone,
a comment, like him,
two parts ill spirited

and one perceptive.

But this night she's
dropped her robe,
come here to be

the kind of woman
who swims naked

without asking
for permission, risking
a stray neighbor

getting the full gander,

buoyed by saltwater,
all the tough and sag
of her softened by

this moonlight's near-
sighted courtesy.

Look at her: how
the woman is floating,

while trying to recall
the exact last
moment of her girlhood—

where she was,
what she was doing—

when she finally

learned what she'd
been taught: to hate

this fleshy sack
of boring anecdotes
and moles she's lived

inside so long,
nemesis without
a zipper for escape.

A pearl is the oyster's

autobiography,
Fellini said. How
clean and weightless

the dive returns
to the woman now;

climbing the high
metal ladder, then

launching herself,
no fear, no notion

of self-preservation,

the arc of her
trajectory pretty
as any arrow's

in Saint Sebastian's
side. How keen
that girl, and sleek,

tumbling more
gorgeous than two
hawks courting

in a dead drop.

Floating, the woman
remembers this again,

how pristine she was
in pike, or tucked
tighter than a socialite, or

twisting in reverse
like a barber's pole,

her body flying
toward its pivot,
which is,

in those seconds,
the Infinite,

before each
possible outcome
tears itself away

(the woman climbing
from the water now)

like the silvery tissue
swaddling a costly
gift.

A Few Notes on the Poems

"Dust thou art, to dust returnest, / Was not spoken of the soul" are lines from Longfellow's poem "A Psalm of Life."

The final two stanzas in "When I Am a Teenage Boy" allude to the opening chapters of *Anna Karenina*.

The epigraph to the poem "Dum Spiro Spero" is a stanza from T. Merrill's poem "Come Lord and Lift."

The poem "Sundays" is written in response to a fifteenth-century Man of Sorrows woodcut, found in the rubble after the 1945 bombing of London. Its German artist is unknown.

The poem "In Which a Therapist Asks for the Gargoyle Who Sits on My Chest" is dedicated to Caryn McCloskey and Dana Levin. Irish-born John O'Neill, referenced in this poem, was a president of the Fenian Brotherhood, an Irish-nationalist secret society in America aiming for Irish independence from Great Britain. With a plan to offer Canadian territories to the British Crown in trade for that independence, Mr. O'Neill executed three failed invasions of Canada from 1866 to 1871, was finally arrested, briefly imprisoned, and ultimately pardoned by Ulysses S. Grant. Mr. O'Neill spent the remainder of his days officially encouraging Irish immigrants to settle land the United

States government offered those hardy souls willing to move to the new state of Nebraska. The town of O'Neill (known as "The Irish Capital of Nebraska") is named after this ill-fated (but remarkably lucky) rebel. If you've ever a chance to spend Saint Patrick's Day in O'Neill, you will, no doubt, enjoy the town's famous celebration.

Sláinte mhaith. *clink*

About the Author

Born in Nebraska, Erin Belieu earned an MA from Boston University and an MFA from Ohio State University. She is the author of four books of poetry: *Infanta* (1995), selected by Hayden Carruth for the National Poetry Series; *One Above & One Below* (2000); *Black Box* (2006), a finalist for the Los Angeles Times Book Prize; and *Slant Six* (2014), a *New York Times* favorite book of 2014. Belieu coedited, with Susan Aizenberg, the anthology *The Extraordinary Tide: New Poetry by American Women* (2001).

Poetry is vital to language and living. Since 1972, Copper Canyon Press has published extraordinary poetry from around the world to engage the imaginations and intellects of readers, writers, booksellers, librarians, teachers, students, and donors.

WE ARE GRATEFUL FOR THE MAJOR SUPPORT PROVIDED BY:

THE PAUL G. ALLEN
FAMILY FOUNDATION

CULTURE

Lannan

A&
OFFICE OF ARTS & CULTURE
SEATTLE

WASHINGTON STATE
ARTS COMMISSION

WE ARE GRATEFUL FOR THE MAJOR SUPPORT PROVIDED BY:

Anonymous

Jill Baker and Jeffrey Bishop

Anne and Geoffrey Barker

Donna and Matthew Bellew

Will Blythe

John Branch

Diana Broze

John R. Cahill

The Beatrice R. and Joseph A. Coleman Foundation

The Currie Family Fund

Laurie and Oskar Eustis

Austin Evans

Saramel Evans

Mimi Gardner Gates

Linda Fay Gerrard

Gull Industries Inc. on behalf of William True

The Trust of Warren A. Gummow

Carolyn and Robert Hedin

Bruce Kahn

Phil Kovacevich and Eric Wechsler

Lakeside Industries Inc. on behalf of Jeanne Marie Lee

Maureen Lee and Mark Busto

Peter Lewis and Johnna Turiano

Ellie Mathews and Carl Youngmann as The North Press

Hank and Liesel Meijer

Jack Nicholson

Gregg Orr

Petunia Charitable Fund and adviser Elizabeth Hebert

Gay Phinny

Suzanne Rapp and Mark Hamilton

Adam and Lynn Rauch

Emily and Dan Raymond

Jill and Bill Ruckelshaus

Cynthia Sears

Kim and Jeff Seely

Joan F. Woods

Barbara and Charles Wright

Caleb Young as C. Young Creative

The dedicated interns and faithful volunteers of Copper Canyon Press

The Chinese character for poetry is made up of two parts:
"word" and "temple." It also serves as pressmark for
Copper Canyon Press.

The poems are set in Sabon.
Book design and composition by Phil Kovacevich.